P9-CDW-026

To Sally and Sue, fellow travelers
C. S.

For Jan Spencer and Paul Miller,
with love
G. B.

Text copyright © 2014 by Claire Saxby
Illustrations copyright © 2014 by Graham Byrne

All rights reserved. No part of this book may be reproduced,
transmitted, or stored in an information retrieval system
in any form or by any means, graphic, electronic, or
mechanical, including photocopying, taping, and recording,
without prior written permission from the publisher.

First U.S. edition 2015

Library of Congress Catalog Card Number 2013957348
ISBN 978-0-7636-7479-3

CCP 20 19 18 17 16 15
10 9 8 7 6 5 4 3 2 1

Printed in Shenzhen, Guangdong, China

This book was typeset in Adobe Garamond Pro and Providence Sans.
The illustrations were created digitally.

Candlewick Press
99 Dover Street
Somerville, Massachusetts 02144

visit us at www.candlewick.com

EMU

CLAIRE SAXBY

ILLUSTRATED BY
GRAHAM BYRNE

CANDLEWICK PRESS

In the open forest, where eucalyptus trees fringe tufty grasslands, honey-pale sunshine seeps to where Emu sits on a nest. Beneath him are eight granite-green eggs. Yes, *him*. For in Emu's world, it is the male's job to raise the fledglings.

Emus can stand as tall as an adult human and weigh 75 to 90 pounds (35 to 40 kilograms). Unlike most birds, emus cannot fly, so they build their nests on the ground.

For months Emu and his mate have danced, sung, and wooed each other. Together they have built a leafy ground nest. Now she perches next to him and lays a final egg. Then she is gone.

Emu gathers the egg under himself and gentles down. His hair-like feathers are soft and will keep the eggs warm. The eggs are large and strong, but without Emu's care, they would perish long before they are ready to hatch.

Once the eggs are laid, female emus have nothing further to do with the hatching or rearing of their young.

As sunshine follows frost, and winds
fetch rain, Emu safeguards his clutch. He
will remain on his nest for eight long weeks,
seldom leaving, even for food or drink.

Nearby, another pair of emus dance.
The forest resounds with their courting calls.
Emu ignores them. They are no threat and
will nest far enough away.

Male emus survive this long period without food or water by limiting their movements and slowing their metabolism, much as hibernating animals do. Even so, they can lose up to 22 pounds (10 kilograms) while they are nesting.

Emu may seem drowsy, but he is not. Today is unusually warm, and winter sleepers stir. He tenses as a goanna approaches. Goannas have stolen his eggs in the past, but not today. Emu watches as the goanna alters her path. Rosellas flit and flutter in the trees.

Then a new voice joins the forest choir. From within an egg, a chick cheeps. The muted call tells Emu his wait is nearly over.

Calling from within the egg hastens the development of other chicks so they will all be born within a few days. The ideal hatching time is late winter, although some chicks may be born in spring.

Over the next week, the first eggs wobble, and
blink-eyed chicks crack their way into their new world.
Gangly, with stippled heads and ribbon stripes,
the chicks survey the forest.

Newly hatched emu chicks are about ten times bigger than a domestic chicken hatchling, but just as vulnerable.

The bold chocolate and cream stripes of their feathers provide effective camouflage in the grasslands.

Emu is ravenous after so long on the nest. He leads the striped chicks to scratch and peck for this first shared meal.

Emu's work is just beginning. His chicks are large and growing fast, but they still need him to keep them warm at night, to protect and teach them. The forest provides food and shelter, but there is also danger.

Only rarely will emus feed their young directly. Mostly the chicks must feed themselves after hatching. An emu's diet consists of fruit, shoots, seeds, and insects.

Emu's chicks dawdle, curious about everything.
The day is fading as they turn to home. A dingo howls,
and Emu grunts an alarm. The chicks squat to the ground,
motionless. They are invisible in the tufty grass.

Emu watches and listens, but the dingo's next howl is
more distant. Even so, Emu gathers the chicks and they
hurry to safety.

Emus are fast, reaching up to 25 miles (40 kilometers) per hour, and can outrun most predators. They will fight only if cornered. Then they peck with their strong beaks or strike out with their clawed feet.

Winter gives way to the promises of spring. The breeze bustles, green and sweet. Stripes give way to mud-murk feathers.

The chicks begin to roam farther as they search for food and explore. Emu keeps a close watch on the ground and the sky.

Emu chicks begin to lose their first feathers when they are three to four months old, although it will be some months before they have their full adult feather coats.

An eagle wheels overhead, casting his dreadful shadow. Emu leads his chicks in a zigzag sprint across the grassland to the safety of the trees.

Emus zigzag to confuse predators. Each change of direction affects the speed and aim of their would-be attackers.

A straggling chick shrieks. He kicks at shadow-wings. The eagle swoops, but Emu is there first. Emu grunts and stiffens his neck. Both his beak and his claws are formidable weapons.

The eagle pulls away in a cacophony of frantic feathers before he feels the force of Emu's strike.

Emus must always be alert to danger.
An emu chick is a valuable prize,
and predators will not give up easily.

Emu's chicks look just like him now, and they are almost his height. But they are still young and not yet ready to survive alone.

Until then, Emu will keep them close.

Young emus are independent from the age of about six months, but it will be more than another year before they are ready to find their own mates.

ABOUT EMUS

Emus are large flightless birds found in Australia. The only bird that is larger than the emu is the ostrich. Emus have three toes, and their feet can be 5½ to 6½ inches (14 to 17 centimeters) long, about as long as a small adult hand. Their wings are too small to do much, although airflow around their wings helps keep them cool when they run.

Emus prefer to live where they are not disturbed by people, but can adapt to a wide range of habitats as long as they have access to water. They are foragers and eat plants and insects. Emus are generally solitary but will travel in large groups to find new sources of water. They are also very inquisitive.

INDEX

DISCARD

Look up the pages to find out about all these emu things.

Don't forget to look at both kinds of words—

this kind and **this kind.**